THIS OR THAT

SURVIVAL

Debate

A RIP-ROARING GAME OF EITHER/OR QUESTIONS

BY ERIK HEINRICH

CAPSTONE PRESS

a capstone imprint

Edge Books are published by Capstone Press,
1710 Roe Crest Drive, North Mankato, Minnesota 56003.
www.capstonepub.com

Library of Congress Cataloging-in-Publication Data
Heinrich, Erik.
This or that survival debate : a rip-roaring game of either-or questions / by Erik
    Heinrich.
p. cm. — (Edge books. This or that?)
Summary: "Offers intriguing either/or questions and content on survival skills and
    situations to encourage critical thinking and debate"—Provided by publisher.
  ISBN 978-1-4296-8594-8 (library binding)
  ISBN 978-1-4296-9278-6 (paperback)
  ISBN 978-1-62065-238-1 (ebook PDF)
1. Logic—Problems, exercises, etc.—Juvenile literature. 2. Critical thinking—
    Problems, exercises, etc.—Juvenile literature. 3. Survival analysis (Biometry)—
    Problems, exercises, etc.—Juvenile literature. 4. Puzzles—Juvenile literature. I.
    Title.
BC108.H35 2013
160—dc23   2012008004

Editorial Credits

Kristen Mohn, editor; Veronica Correia, designer; Eric Gohl, media researcher;
    Laura Manthe, production specialist

Photo Credits

Art Parts: Ron and Joe, Inc., cover (all); Corbis: Bettmann, 1; Dreamstime: Pascalou95,
27; iStockphotos: Graeme Whittle, 4, Peter Jochems, 8 (bottom), supakitmod, 25
(right); Newscom: akg-images, 6, CMSP Education/Custom Medical Stock Photo/
Nawrocki Stock Photo, 7, Danita Delimont Photography/DanitaDelimont.com/Alan
Klehr, 10, EPA/Lechner/HBF, 14, Getty Images/AFP/HO, 5; Shutterstock: AJancso,
9 (bottom), Alessandro Campagnolo, 26, Alexander Dashewsky, 16 (front), Andreas
Gradin, 8 (top), Dale Mitchell, 23, Daniel Alvarez, 19, Germanskydiver, 22, Igumnova
Irina, 29, Irina_QQQ, cover & interior (background), Jhaz Photography, 28, John
Hoadley, 20 (front), Maitree Laipitaksin, 9 (top), mastiffliu, 21 (back), mrfiza, 12, Ozja,
18, Patryk Kosmider, 21 (front), Peter Bay, 3, 13, Peter J. Wilson, 15, Photosani, 17,
Richard Peterson, 24 (left), Scott E Read, 24–25, Todd Shoemake, 11, Valentyn Volkov,
16 (back); Super Stock Inc.: Photononstop, 20 (back)

Printed in the United States of America in Stevens Point, Wisconsin.
032012   006678WZF12

How to Use This Book:

Avalanches or wildfires? Quicksand or thin ice? Choose the survival challenges you'd rather face. The questions in this book place you in dangerous situations with wild animals, extreme nature, and other hazards. Whether it's sailing with pirates or swimming with crocodiles, you'll get to call the shots. Read the questions, weigh the options, and then decide—what would you choose?

When you are finished reading the book, try some questions on your family and friends. What would they choose? Are their answers different from yours? If so, debate!

THIS

- dangerously hot sand
- deadly spiders and snakes
- possibility of unfriendly inhabitants

On many islands, venomous spiders and snakes are real dangers. For example, the venom of a banded sea krait can kill a person in just six hours. While avoiding the wildlife, you have to worry about super hot beach sand blistering your feet. There is also a small chance of running into unfriendly local people who may take you prisoner. On the bright side, some islands have coconuts that contain white meat and milky water that will keep you alive. And you can use beach wood or rocks to spell out SOS for an airplane to spot.

OR THAT?

TO BE LOST AT SEA IN A RUBBER RAFT WITH A FLARE GUN

In sunny tropical seas you could develop heatstroke in a matter of minutes without shade. Heatstroke can result in organ failure and death. There is also the slight chance a shark will take a test bite of your raft and sink you—or eat you. But if you survive long enough, ocean currents may carry you to a seaport. Or you may be rescued by a ship or plane passing your way. When you spot the rescue vehicle, you can fire your flare gun to get the crew's attention.

- heatstroke dangers
- possibility of a shark attack
- might sink in rough seas

THIS

TO BE CAPTURED 200 YEARS AGO

BY CARIBBEAN PIRATES

- known to be killers
- attack ships
- torture prisoners

Famous pirate captains like Blackbeard and Henry Morgan were always on the lookout for ships to rob. Especially valuable were pieces of eight, which were Spanish dollar coins from the late 1400s. Pirates were rough characters who thought nothing of killing anyone they battled. In addition to treasure, pirates would also take hostages, chain them, and hold them for ransom. If the pirates didn't like a hostage and couldn't get a ransom, the victim would be killed. Then he'd be sent to "Davy Jones' Locker"—the bottom of the sea.

OR THAT?

TO BE CAPTURED 200 YEARS AGO BY SOUTH PACIFIC HEADHUNTERS

- stalk victims
- chop off heads
- keep slaves

Headhunting is the practice of taking a person's head after he or she has been killed as part of a ceremony or ritual. As recently as a century ago, headhunting was common among some people in Borneo, the Philippines, and Papua New Guinea. The main reason for keeping an enemy's head was as a trophy that proved a warrior's success in battle. Some headhunters also practiced cannibalism, which means the rest of your body would have been their dinner. If they spared your life, you would likely have become a slave.

THIS

RIVER WITH PIRANHAS

- fast swimmers
- razor-sharp teeth
- eat victims alive

Piranhas are small South American fish that live in lakes and rivers. Luckily, they rarely bite humans. But if they do, the resulting blood will start a feeding frenzy. You will suddenly find yourself surrounded by hundreds of these aggressive fish. A swarm of piranhas is able to eat all the flesh from a human in minutes, leaving only a skeleton. Your chance of escaping such an attack is next to zero.

OR THAT?

RIVER WITH CAIMANS

- up to 8 feet (2.4 meters) long
- crushing bites
- drown victims

Similar to the American alligator, the caiman is a water reptile found in Central and South America. If you are attacked by a young caiman there's a small chance you might be able to get away. However, if a full-grown caiman has you in its powerful jaws, you are almost certain to meet a watery death. A caiman has long rows of sharp teeth that can bite off an arm or leg. But it's most likely to drown you before beginning its meal.

THIS

TO BE IN A HURRICANE WARNING AREA

- dangerous storm surges
- chance to evacuate
- deadliest U.S. hurricane killed more than 6,000 people

With wind speeds of more than 160 miles (257 kilometers) per hour, hurricanes can damage a wide area of buildings, trees, and cars. When a hurricane hits land, it can dump more than 2.4 trillion gallons (9 trillion liters) of rain per day. This rain, along with giant waves called storm surges, floods cities and causes serious damage. The good news is that hurricanes can usually be predicted several days before they hit. Residents often have time to leave the area and save their lives, if not their homes.

OR THAT?

TO BE IN A
TORNADO
WARNING AREA

- little time to seek shelter
- over in minutes
- kill about 60 people per year in the United States

Meteorologists can usually give people only about 11 minutes of warning that a tornado may strike. Getting to a basement or windowless interior room is the best chance of survival if a tornado hits. That's because the biggest threat from a tornado is getting hit by debris swirling in the wind. The strongest tornadoes have estimated wind speeds of 300 miles (483 km) per hour. This wind is powerful enough to tear down a house or throw a car across the street like a soda can. A community can be flattened by a tornado in minutes.

THIS

TO GET A MOSQUITO BITE

- hard to avoid
- many mosquitoes carry diseases
- can be deadly

In tropical countries, mosquitoes spread deadly diseases such as malaria and yellow fever. As a result, the mosquito kills more humans each year than any other animal worldwide. More than 700,000 people die from malaria every year. Vaccinations can provide protection. Mosquito nets over beds can also help. In North America and other countries, mosquitoes can carry the dangerous West Nile virus. But cases of West Nile are very rare. It's much more likely you'll just end up with an itchy bite.

OR THAT?

TO GET A
SCORPION
STING

- sneaky
- stinger on tail
- chance of deadly venom

The scorpion is a relative of the spider. Its tail has a venomous, needlelike stinger. Commonly thought to be desert dwellers, scorpions can also live in rain forests and other places around the world. There are nearly 2,000 species. The good news is that only 30 to 40 species carry venom strong enough to kill a human. Scorpions like to burrow in soil, which makes them difficult to spot. A scorpion is not likely to sting you unless you accidentally step on it. But even if the sting is not deadly, it's going to hurt more than a mosquito bite.

13

THIS

TO GET CAUGHT IN AN AVALANCHE

- unpredictable
- unstoppable
- deadliest U.S. avalanche killed 96 people

An avalanche happens when a huge shelf of ice or snow breaks off a mountainside. The snow and other materials race down at speeds up to 200 miles (322 km) per hour. Avalanches often happen without warning and can bury entire towns in minutes. If an avalanche is coming at you, your best chance of survival is to try to move out of its path. If you're buried, try to create an air pocket near your face so that you can breathe. If possible, raise a hand above the snow to flag rescuers.

OR THAT?

TO GET CAUGHT IN A WILDFIRE

- fires cover a lot of territory quickly
- difficult to stop
- deadliest forest fire in U.S. history killed 1,152 people

If you find yourself close to a forest fire, you may be in serious trouble. The flames are dangerous, but the leading cause of death with forest fires is breathing in the smoke. The best chance of survival is to crouch low on a barren patch of earth. Clear wood and other flammable material away from you. Scooping loose dirt onto your body may give you some protection. Forest fires can spread as fast as 14 miles (23 km) per hour. At this speed, fires can cover thousands of acres quickly.

THIS

With a box of matches you can light a bonfire. Smoke from the fire may help someone locate you. At night a fire will keep you warm. Predators such as bears and wolves see fire as a danger and will keep away. This is especially important at night when you are unable to see in the dark. But beware—9 out of 10 forest fires are caused by humans.

- provides light and warmth
- scares away animals
- must use with caution— fires spread quickly

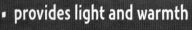

OR THAT?

IF YOU'RE LOST IN THE FOREST... TO HAVE A COMPASS

- compact
- reliable
- requires some knowledge to use

A compass is a great tool—but it's only helpful if you know which compass direction you need to go. Once you know where you're headed, a compass will keep you on the right track. But if your compass doesn't have a light, you won't be able to read it in the dark. That might mean a cold, dangerous night in the woods.

THIS

TO ENCOUNTER A
SABER-TOOTHED
TIGER FROM HISTORY

- biggest cat in history
- giant fangs
- killer claws

The saber-toothed tiger lived more than 10,000 years ago. It had curving canine teeth called sabers that were nearly 12 inches (30 centimeters) long. The South American species was the biggest feline to ever walk the Earth. It weighed as much as 1,000 pounds (454 kilograms). This killer cat jumped on its victims from the branches of trees. Then it dug its sabers into the victim's neck for a fast kill.

TO ENCOUNTER A SPOTTED HYENA TODAY

- aggressive
- eats prey dead or alive
- shakes small prey to death

The spotted hyena is a skilled hunter and scavenger from Africa and Asia. It's built like a bear and has powerful jaws that can crush bones to a pulp. Hyenas hunt in groups and are able to take down animals larger than themselves. They will chase prey for miles and can run as fast as 35 miles (56 km) per hour. For that reason, trying to run away from a hungry hyena is a bad idea. Standing your ground and looking as big as possible may convince the hyena to leave you alone.

THIS

INTO QUICKSAND

- hard to spot
- heavy and thick
- can be a deadly trap

Quicksand is a hidden danger that could be deadly. It's very rare to drown in quicksand, but it's extremely hard to get out of. The danger is that you'll get trapped there and no one will find you for days. By then you may be dead from thirst or cold. The best chance of survival is to lean back in a spread-eagle position and slowly wiggle toward firm ground. If you're lucky, a passerby will pull you out with a walking stick or rope.

DANGER
QUICKSAND
DO NOT
ENTER

TO FALL THROUGH THIN ICE

- thickness of ice hard to determine
- freezing cold
- high risk of drowning

On impact with cold water you will feel as if someone has knocked the breath out of you. As a result there is a danger of filling your lungs with water when you draw your first breath. It's difficult to swim in winter clothing and the cold water will make you even more sluggish. There's a high chance of drowning if you slip under the ice sheet. Without rescue, you will be unconscious in less than 15 minutes.

DANGER
STAY OFF
THE ICE
DEEP WATER

THIS

TO BAIL OUT OF A
BURNING AIRPLANE
WITH A PARACHUTE

- difficult to navigate
- parachute may not open
- impact on landing could be deadly

If you know how to use it, a parachute may save you from a burning plane. But it may not save your life. If the wind blows you into a tree or electrical lines, there's nothing you can do about it. If you're lucky you will have a soft landing in a farmer's field or a city park. If you're unlucky you might land in the middle of a lake or on top of a snowy mountain.

TO FALL INTO AN
ICE CREVASSE
WITH CLIMBING GEAR

- freezing temperatures
- may be 100 feet (30 m) deep
- chance of breaking leg or arm in fall

A crevasse is a deep crack in the surface of a glacier caused by ice flowing over uneven ground. Climbing out of a crevasse will be hard, especially if you have injured yourself in the fall. The jagged walls will make it difficult to use a pick axe or climbing boots with spikes. Hopefully, the opening near the top of the crevasse will be narrow enough to stop your fall. That will make for a shorter climb to safety—as long as you aren't wedged too tightly.

THIS

DEFEND YOURSELF AGAINST A MOUNTAIN LION WITH A BULLWHIP

- tricky to handle
- may end up injuring yourself
- does not need to make contact with an animal to work

A bullwhip is a long braided whip originally used to control cattle and livestock. It makes a loud cracking sound that startles animals. That's why circus lion tamers use it. The sound of a bullwhip is likely to scare a mountain lion and most other predators away. But a bullwhip can do little real harm. At most it tears flesh—including the handler's if not used correctly.

OR THAT?

DEFEND YOURSELF AGAINST A MOUNTAIN LION WITH A

SLINGSHOT

- fast
- needs to be reloaded
- accurate—if you are experienced

A slingshot is a small handheld weapon that can kill a small animal. A well-aimed shot can startle and possibly wound a lion. This might convince the animal to stay away. Or it could make it angry and result in a deadly revenge attack. Since a slingshot has to be loaded, aimed, and fired, it is not very useful if the animal surprises you at close range.

THIS

TO BE LOOKING FOR WATER IN THE ARIZONA DESERT

- some vegetation and trees
- ranger stations
- wild animals

If you can't find fresh water in the Arizona Desert, you still have a pretty good chance of finding a barrel cactus. This large prickly plant has moisture inside. As a general rule it's not a good idea to drink cactus juice because it contains chemicals that can cause diarrhea. But in an emergency it can save your life. In the best-case scenario you will stumble across a ranger station and be rescued. In the worst-case scenario, you'll stumble upon a rattlesnake.

BARREL CACTUS

TO BE LOOKING FOR WATER IN THE SAHARA DESERT

- huge
- dry riverbeds
- desert tribes

Spreading across the entire continent, the Sahara is the biggest desert in Africa. Dry riverbeds are an important source of emergency water in the Sahara. These riverbeds sometimes contain pockets of moisture just a few feet below the surface. But there aren't many riverbeds in the Sahara, and they are difficult to spot. If you are lucky, you might find a local tribe who will give you water.

THIS

TO GET CAUGHT IN A LIGHTNING STORM

- heavy rain
- tall objects may attract lightning
- lightning is the leading cause of weather-related injury

Lightning releases its electrical charge into the nearest object it can find. The nearest object is usually also the tallest. That's why taking shelter under a tree or bridge increases your chances of being struck by lightning. There are an average of 55 reported lightning fatalities each year in the United States. About 10 percent of people who are struck by lightning are killed. The other 90 percent have various injuries, some very severe. The chance of being struck by lightning once in your life is 1 in 10,000.

OR THAT?

TO GET CAUGHT IN A BLIZZARD

- low visibility causes car accidents
- high winds
- freezing cold and risk of hypothermia

In 1888 a record-setting blizzard in the eastern United States killed more than 400 people. A blizzard comes with powerful winds that can reach 100 miles (161 km) per hour. Blowing snow can make it difficult to see while driving. Slick roads and drifting snow can cause deadly accidents or trap you in your vehicle. Without shelter, there is the possibility of dying from hypothermia. Hypothermia occurs when a person's core temperature drops below 95 degrees Fahrenheit (35 degrees Celsius). With hypothermia, shivering and confusion can progress to death within an hour or two.

Lightning Round:

▶ Would you choose to hide in a COFFIN SWARMING WITH MICE or a LOCKER CRAWLING WITH COCKROACHES?

▶ Would you choose to be a SMOKEJUMPER or a GHOST HUNTER?

▶ Would you choose to lose control of a HANG GLIDER or a MOTORCYCLE?

▶ Would you choose to run from VOLCANIC LAVA or from a TSUNAMI?

▶ Would you choose to eat DUNG BEETLES or LOCUSTS to survive?

▶ Would you choose to jump off a RUNNING HORSE or a MOVING TRAIN?

▶ Would you choose to be trapped on an ELEVATOR or in an AIRPLANE BATHROOM?

▶ Would you choose to be lost in the JUNGLE or a STRANGE CITY at night?

▶ Would you choose to CLIMB MOUNT EVEREST or COMPLETE A SOLO SAIL AROUND THE WORLD?

▶ Would you choose to be a BIG GAME HUNTER IN AFRICA or an INTERNATIONAL SPY?

▶ Would you choose to LOSE THE USE OF YOUR LEGS WHILE SWIMMING or LOSE YOUR VISION WHILE DOWNHILL SKIING?

▶ Would you choose to SLEEP IN A TREE IN A JUNGLE or ON A MOUNTAIN LEDGE?

▶ Would you choose to drink YOUR URINE or DIRTY RIVER WATER in an emergency?

▶ Would you choose to live through the MOUNT VESUVIUS VOLCANO ERUPTION IN AD 79 or THE SPANISH FLU OF 1918-1919?

▶ Would you choose to be STUCK IN A WELL or LOST IN A CAVE?

▶ Would you choose to get BURNS or FROSTBITE?

▶ Would you choose to RUN OUT OF GAS ON A DESERTED ROAD or FIND A HOLE IN YOUR BOAT IN THE MIDDLE OF A LAKE?

▶ Would you choose to be a TORNADO CHASER or a HURRICANE HUNTER?

▶ Would you choose to fight in a duel using FENCING or GRECO-ROMAN WRESTLING?

Read More

Campbell, Guy. *The Boys' Book of Survival: How To Survive Anything, Anywhere.* New York: Scholastic, 2009.

Hunter, Nick. *Surviving Disasters.* Extreme Survival. Chicago: Raintree, 2011.

Long, Denise. *Survivor Kid: A Practical Guide to Wilderness Survival.* Chicago: Chicago Review Press, 2011.

O'Shei, Tim. *How to Survive in the Wilderness.* Prepare to Survive. Mankato, Minn.: Capstone Press, 2009.

Internet Sites

FactHound offers a safe, fun way to find Internet sites related to this book. All of the sites on FactHound have been researched by our staff.

Here's all you do:

Visit *www.facthound.com*

Type in this code: 9781429685948

Super-cool stuff! Check out projects, games and lots more at
www.capstonekids.com